BAKING FOR DOGS

THE BEST RECIPES FROM DOG'S DELI

FRIEDERIKE FRIEDEL

With Photographs by Thomas Schultze

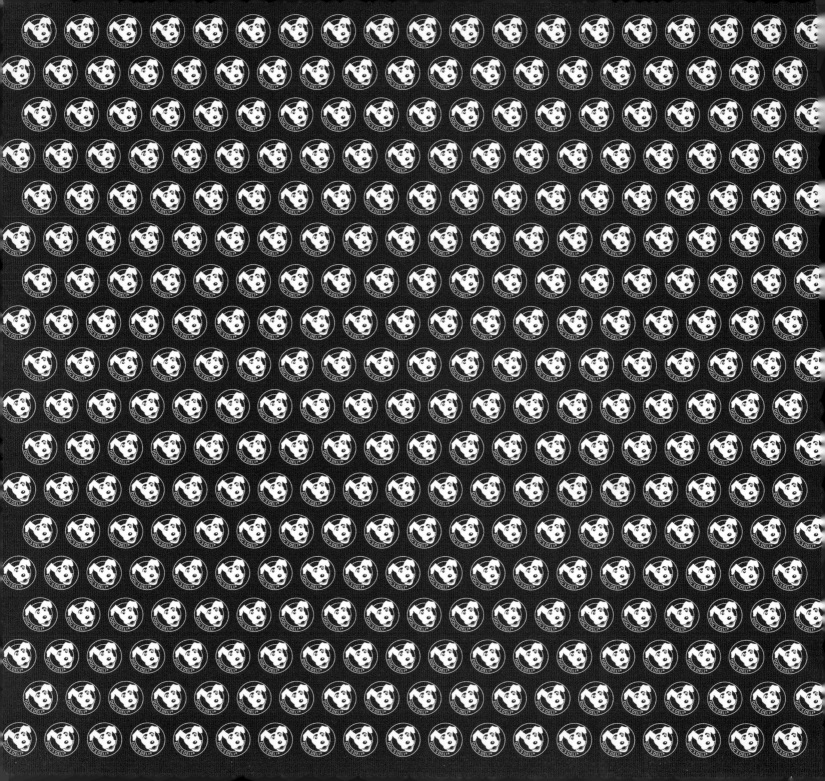

Text: Friederike Friedel
Photos: Thomas Schultze
Setup and Formation: Claudia Renierkens, renierkens kommunikations-design, Cologne
Editor: Vera Brunn
Reader: Petra Hundacker
Translation: Ed Force

This cookbook was written according to the author's best knowledge and intent. Neither the publisher nor the author bears the responsibility for unwanted reactions or opinions that arise from using the ingredients. The recipes may not be utilized for business use.

Originally published in Germany by HEEL Verlag GmbH as **Backen Fur Hunde**

Copyright © 2009 by Schiffer Publishing Ltd.
Library of Congress Control Number: 2009925207

Type set in Humanist 521 UBld/Humanist 521 BT

ISBN: 978-0-7643-3248-7
Printed in China

Schiffer Books are available at special discounts for bulk purchases for sales promotions or premiums. Special editions, including personalized covers, corporate imprints, and excerpts can be created in large quantities for special needs. For more information contact the publisher:

Published by Schiffer Publishing Ltd.
4880 Lower Valley Road
Atglen, PA 19310
Phone: (610) 593-1777; Fax: (610) 593-2002
E-mail: Info@schifferbooks.com

For the largest selection of fine reference books on this and related subjects, please visit our web site at **www.schifferbooks.com**
We are always looking for people to write books on new and related subjects. If you have an idea for a book please contact us at the above address.

This book may be purchased from the publisher.
Include $5.00 for shipping.
Please try your bookstore first.
You may write for a free catalog.

In Europe, Schiffer books are distributed by
Bushwood Books
6 Marksbury Ave.
Kew Gardens
Surrey TW9 4JF England
Phone: 44 (0) 20 8392 8585; Fax: 44 (0) 20 8392 9876
E-mail: info@bushwoodbooks.co.uk
Website: www.bushwoodbooks.co.uk

CONTENTS

DOG'S DELI®

Watermaniacs Beachboy Bill, called Billy, is a brown male Labrador who was the inspiration for DOG'S DELI®. If he would not eat so willingly and thus were not so simple to train or to bribe, as some would say, who knows whether the idea for our business would ever have been born.

DOG'S DELI is a bakery for dogs' baked goods in Carlstadt, Duesseldorf, Germany. We bake fresh there every day, and much testing and talking is done. Our customers ask again and again for certain recipes—the best inspiration for the DOG'S DELI team to invent a new cookie.

Baking by following recipes from DOG'S DELI is child's play. As a matter of principle, neither sugar nor additives, fragrances nor readymade products are used. You probably have most of the ingredients on hand at home. If you should get hungry yourself, go ahead and take a bite of one of your fresh-baked cookies.

And even if your cookies don't look just like the ones in our pictures, don't be too hard on yourself. In such a case, we at DOG'S DELI always smile and say: "After all, they are only dog cookies." And they always taste good to your dog, no matter how successful they look to you.

1

2

3

4

5

6

1. Bananas
2. Dogs
3. Miss Swiss
4. Wild Hearts
5. Lucky Pigs
6. Rabbit Food
7. Muscle Builders
8. Prince on the Pea

Not all our cookies would fit into the book. They can be had at DOG'S DELI. Or maybe in the next edition.

7

8

Your home-baked dog cookies are something special, really a delicacy. Feed them to your dog as a reward or a little snack. And even though they are so delicious, Billy only gets to enjoy them now and then, and thus with twice the joy.

Never bake too much at once. **Fresh** tastes best to every dog. The recipes are made up so that they make about a two-week supply. The dog cookies last for a limited time, since no preservatives are included, so it is best to keep them in a tin box or linen bag, so that they can dry. Or share them with your dog's girl friend in the park.

Should your dog have a **food allergy,** discuss the recipe with your veterinarian before you use it. Sometimes changing one ingredient, such as the type of flour, is the solution and you will have developed a suitable cookie just for your dog.

Naturally, Billy has been the first dog to sample all the recipes and found his very own **favorites.** The dogs who are our clients at **DOG'S DELI** have tested and criticized many recipes and thus contributed to improvements in the recipe book.

Variation in feeding is the secret.

A Word about Measuring Ingredients

In Germany we measure most ingredients by weight, not volume, in part because we have found it convenient and accurate. We have given measurements in both grams and the pound equivalents. A small kitchen scale should make it easy to measure in this way. We have also included the volume equivalent for the various ingredients, for the reader's convenience.

TIP
And so you can also impress your dog with new training ideas every day, Billy's dog trainer from the "Knochenarbeit" (Very Hard Work) dog school has written a **training tip** for every day.

Billy

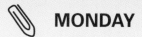

A DAY AT THE OFFICE

The first day of the week always begins with great excitement. Every Monday at 10:00 Billy has a swimming lesson in a real swimming pool that is reserved just for dogs. Hard to believe? What fun it is for him to swim with the physiotherapist and retrieve dummies. Good for the muscles and joints, good for his mood— and very, very tiring.

Thus Monday, usually rather boring, is easier to get through. The DOG'S DELI is closed, so there is plenty of time for shopping, appointments, and office work, but alas, without dog friends. Sleeping, waiting, sleeping; no, it isn't exactly a dream day for a Labrador. Billy waits patiently in the car at the supermarket or the bank, or waits in the office.

Tasty morsels shorten Billy's waiting time, bring variety and occupy his attention. His favorite cookies are the Amarettini. Amarettini are wrapped in paper, and so his excitement lasts longer.

For Monday we offer you three recipes for treats that preserve good moods.

BILLY'S TIME-PASSING TIP
There must not be boredom!
Pack your dog a few tasty cookies in empty cardboard boxes. Hide them in your home and then let him look for them. In the beginning, your dog can watch you happily. It gets harder when the boxes are hidden in secret. After a successful search, your dog can either unpack the cookies himself or retrieve the boxes so you can open them for him.

AMARETTINI

Ingredients	How to do it
2-1/2 cups (9 oz or 250 g) rye flour 2/3 cup (2 oz or 50 g) ground hazel nuts 1/2 cup (2 oz or 50 g) ground almonds 1/2 cup (4.5 oz or 125 g) fat free yogurt 1 tablespoon honey 4 tablespoons (50 ml) sunflower oil About 1/3 cup (75 ml) water	1. Preheat oven to 300° F and line baking pan with baking paper. 2. Measure and mix rye flour, hazel nuts and almonds. 3. Add fat free yogurt, honey, sunflower oil and water. 4. Stir everything well and form balls some 2 cm in diameter. 5. Cut the balls in half with a knife and lay them on the sheet. 6. Bake about 20 minutes at 300° F. 7. Let amarettinis cool. 8. Cut squares, about 4" x 4", of the tissue paper and wrap the individual cookies in them.

Utensils
One roll of tissue paper

TIP Add the water only bit by bit at the end. If the dough gets too sticky, add some rye flour.

Billy loves to unwrap the amarettinis himself. And remarkably, he eats only the cookies. Then he tears up the tissue paper with great pleasure.

First baked on:

DOG'SDELI®

w.dogsdeli.de

VALENTINE HEARTS

Ingredients	How to do it
2-1/2 cups (8 oz or 250 g) wheat flour 1 cup (3.5 oz or 100 g) oat bran. 1 cup (1/4 lb or 100 g) fresh raspberries 1 tablespoon honey Marrow of one vanilla bean 2 tablespoons (25 ml) sunflower oil About 1 cup (200 ml) warm water	1. Preheat oven to 300° F and line baking pan with baking paper. 2. Measure and mix wheat flour and oat bran. 3. Cut vanilla bean lengthwise, take out marrow and add to flour 4. Gradually add washed raspberries, honey, sunflower oil and water. 5. Mix it to a smooth dough with a hand or electric mixer. 6. Roll the dough to about 1/4" thickness on a floured work surface and cut out hearts with a cookie cutter. 7. Lay the cookies on a cookie sheet. 8. Bake 25 minutes at 300° F.
Utensils	
Rolling pin, heart-shaped cookie cutter	

TIP: You can also use frozen raspberries. Let the berries thaw in a small bowl. Reduce the amount of water in the recipe and add the berry juice instead.

First baked on:

PEANUT STRUDEL

Ingredients	How to do it
Light Dough: 2 cups (9 oz or 250 g) wheat flour 2 tablespoons (25 ml) sunflower oil About 150 ml water **Dark Dough:** 1-1/2 cups (7 oz or 200 g) wheat flour 1 cup (3.5 oz or 100 g) ground peanuts 1 tablespoon maple syrup 2 tablespoons (25 ml) sunflower oil About 1/2 cup (100 ml) water	1. Preheat oven to 325° F and line baking pan with baking paper. 2. Measure wheat flour and peanuts for light and dark dough and mix well in two bowls. 3. Gradually add sunflower oil, maple syrup and water. 4. Mix to smooth doughs with a hand or electric mixer. 5. Roll out light and dark dough some 1/8" thick and lay one on top of the other. 6. Cut dough into strips about 3/8" wide and 1" long. 7. Roll the dough strips into small spirals and put them on the baking pan. 8. Bake about 25 minutes at 325° F.
Utensils Rolling pin	

Variations   Instead of maple syrup, you can also use honey, and hazel nuts or walnuts are a variation on peanuts.

Billy spent his first hours outdoors under a walnut tree in a meadow with his mother and siblings. Fee, his lovely mother, cracked fresh walnuts into her whelps' mouths. This is probably why Billy has such a fondness for walnuts.

First baked on:

Emily

IN THE BAKERY

A day at DOG'S DELI begins for Billy with fresh water in his bowl and a bone to chew on. At 10:00 the bakery is opened, and from then on he lies on his pillow in the office and observes every dog and owner who comes in.

Emily, Nele and other lovely ladies may visit him in the office. Billy shares fresh cookies, straight from the cookie sheet, with them. Sometimes secretly too, or so he thinks.

His greatest pleasure is when "Schmankerl" treats are baked. They are our little croissants, filled with liverwurst. If liverwurst should be left over, he can lick it right out of the big glass, a great ten-minute job. Of course this does not happen every Tuesday.

In the afternoon he goes for a walk in the nearby park. Finally he gets out and smells who has been in the neighborhood and might come to DOG'S DELI.

At 6:30 the shop is closed, and a long day has been survived. PUH.

BILLY'S OBEDIENCE TIP

Lying well-behaved on the blanket

Let your dog make a bed on his blanket and put a reward between his forepaws when he settles down. Step just one step back from your dog at first. Go right back to him and reward him again on the blanket when he remains lying there. Then increase the difficulty by gradually increasing the distance from the blanket. Reward your dog when he lies there, quiet and well-behaved, even when you turn away.

On Tuesday we offer you three recipes that you can vary according to your own imagination.

CROSSIES

Ingredients	How to do it
2-1/2 cups (7 oz or 200 g) coarse oatmeal 1-1/2 cups (4.5 oz or 125 g) fine oatmeal 1 cup (3.5 oz or 100 g) shredded coconut, unsweetened 1/2 cup (100 ml) milk 1/8 cup (25 ml) sunflower oil 2 eggs	1. Preheat oven to 350° F and line baking pan with baking paper. 2. Measure and mix oatmeal and coconut flakes. 3. Add milk, eggs and sunflower oil. 4. Mix it all well. 5. Make small spheres, about 3/4" in diameter, by hand. 6. Lay the crossies on the cookie sheet. 7. Bake for about 25 minutes at 350° F and then let them dry well for several hours.

TIP Rinse your fingers now and then while making the crossies. Then the dough will not stick so much.

Variation

Replace the coconut flakes with 2 ounces of cut-up fresh zucchini or 2 ounces of grated carrots. The crossies also taste great with fresh cut-up fruit in season, such as apricots or strawberries. You should use them up within a week.

First baked on:

SUMMER MUFFINS

Ingredients	How to do it
3-1/2 cups (3/4 lb or 350 g) rye flour 1 level teaspoon of baking powder 1 cup (1/3 lb or 150 g) straw-berries 3 eggs 1/3 cup (75 ml) milk 1/4 cup (50 ml) sunflower oil	1. Preheat oven to 350° F and grease the muffin pan with a little sunflower oil. 2. Measure rye flower and mix with baking powder. 3. Puree the washed strawberries. Naturally, you can use a mixer. You can also cut them into small pieces with a knife. 4. Add pureed berries, eggs, milk and sunflower oil to the flour. 5. Stir it all well and put the dough into the muffin pan. 6. Bake about 20 minutes at 1350° F . Poke a muffin with a toothpick. If a little dough still sticks to it, bake the muffins a few more minutes.

Utensils
Muffin pan (8 muffins) or paper forms Hand mixer

TIP Muffins should not be kept longer than four days. You can also freeze them and defrost them for special occasions.

Variation

Replace the strawberries with a fresh banana or pureed apple. Billy especially loves muffins when they are made hearty. You can also use 1/3 lb of grated Swiss cheese or shredded carrots as a delicious alternative.

First baked on:

BLUEBERRY SCONES

Ingredients	How to do it
1-2/3 cups (7 oz or 200 g) wheat flour 1-1/2 cups (4.4 oz or 125 g) coarse oatmeal 1 level teaspoon of baking powder 3/4 cups (3.5 oz or 100 g) blueberries 2 eggs 1/2 cup (4.4 oz or 125 g) fat-free yogurt 1/4 cup (50 ml) sunflower oil	1. Preheat oven to 350° F . 2. Measure wheat flour and oatmeal and mix with baking powder. 3. Add eggs, yogurt and sunflower oil and stir well. 4. Carefully add the washed blueberries. 5. Take off clumps with a tablespoon and place on the baking pan. 6. Bake about 25 minutes at 350° F . Stick a toothpick into a scone. If dough still sticks to it, bake the scones a few more minutes.

TIP For a small dog, use a teaspoon and make small scones. The baking time should then be reduced to 20 minutes.

Variation
Replace the blueberries with a fresh pureed banana. Reduce the oatmeal by 1/2 cup and use coarsely chopped hazel nuts or peanuts in place of it.

First baked on:

A DAY WITH THE DOG-SITTER

On Wednesday Billy has a date with his dog-sitter, and he loves him. Somehow I have the feeling that everything revolves around him. And for a Labrador, that is always the nicest moment.

It starts about noon. A long walk in the woods, where one does not always meet just friends. Always these ill-bred mutts, these bad boys. Usually they are mutts whom Billy does not like. Well, maybe the feeling is mutual.

At least such meetings have one big advantage. There are the best treats for distraction. For them, he naturally concentrates on his two-legged friend.

BILLY'S FITNESS TIP
Fun in the Woods
Tree trunks and other barriers in the woods are very good for training in coordination and balance. Let your dog balance himself along fallen tree trunks or jump over them. Lure him into crawling under barriers, such as a park bench, or let him SIT on a tree stump. To reward the "trick" and encourage cleverness, liver dumplings, salmon cookies and Bill's Best are especially suitable.

Recipes for treats like liver dumplings, salmon cookies and Bill's Best are found on the following pages.

LIVER DUMPLINGS

Ingredients	How to do it
2-1/2 cups (1/2 lb or 250 g) rye flour	1. Preheat the oven to 340° F and line the baking pan with baking paper.
1/3 lb (150 g) fresh chicken liver	2. Cook chicken liver in water about 15 minutes and let it cool.
2 tablespoons chopped parsley	3. Puree chicken liver with water.
3-1/2 tablespoons (50 ml) sunflower oil	4. Measure rye flour.
About 1/2 cup (125 ml) water	5. Add pureed chicken liver, parsley and oil and stir to a smooth dough.
	6. Make small balls, about 3/4" in diameter, with your fingers.
Utensils	7. Bake about 25 minutes at 340° F .
Cooking pot, hand mixer	

TIP Instead of 1/2 cup of tap water, you can also use 1/2 cup of chicken-liver broth.

Billy thinks liver dumplings are great. But it is not my favorite recipe. They do not smell as good when they are baking as the other treats do. So be sure to ventilate well.

First baked on:

SALMON COOKIES

Ingredients	How to do it
2-1/2 cups (11 oz or 300 g) wheat flour 2/3 cup (2 oz or 50 g) soft oatmeal 1/2 lb (200 g) raw salmon fillet 1 egg 3-1/2 tablespoons (50 ml) sunflower oil About 1/2 cup (100 ml) water	1. Preheat oven to 300° F and line baking pan with baking paper. 2. Cook salmon fillet in water for 15 minutes and let it cool. 3. Puree fish with water. 4. Measure and mix wheat flour and oatmeal. 5. Add the salmon, egg, and sunflower oil. 6. Mix everything to a smooth dough with a hand or electric mixer. 7. Roll the dough to about 1/4" thickness on a floured surface and cut out fish with a cookie cutter. 8. Put the cookies on the sheet and bake them about 20 minutes at 300° F .

Utensils
Mixer, cooking pot, rolling pin, fish cookie cutter

Variations

You can also use tuna. Canned tuna is very suitable.
If possible, use a type packed in water.

First baked on:

BILL'S BEST

Ingredients	How to do it
1-1/3 cups (6 oz or 180 g) yellow cornmeal 2/3 cup (2.5 or 75 g) wheat flour 1 banana 1 egg 1/2 cup (2 oz or 50 g) ground walnuts 2 tablespoons (25 ml) sunflower oil	1. Preheat oven to 320° F and line baking pan with baking paper. 2. Weigh and mix cornmeal, wheat flour and walnuts. 3. Mash banana with fork and add to the flour mixture. 4. Add the egg and sunflower oil 5. Mix to a smooth dough with a hand or electric mixer. Maybe add warm water. 6. Roll the dough about 1/4" thick on a floured surface. 7. Cut small cubes (about 1/4" x 1/4" with a large knife. 8. Put the cubes on the baking pan and bake about 20 minutes at 320° F .
Utensils	
Rolling pin	

Variation
Instead of walnuts, you can use chopped hazel nuts.

Billy hates fresh bananas. But he eats them gladly in these cookies. Or maybe he doesn't smell them?

First baked on:

AT THE DOG SCHOOL

On Thursday Billy has an important appointment.

Whether he sees it that way is naturally a big question. An hour at "Knochenarbeit", his dog school in Duesseldorf, demands the highest concentration from him. Very much a strain, but a whole hour long for both of us, real "bone work".

One could really get the impression that Billy can do everything. And only I, the human, must learn to communicate with him. School for dogs or masters? In any case, all success is rewarded with praise and an especially delicious training treat.

It is really astounding how well Billy can behave there. In the everyday world he sometimes has forgotten so much. Funny.

BILLY'S TRAINING TIP
Concentration in every life situation
Honor every spontaneous eye contact of your dog with you with a treat. **Distance**: Hold a dog cookie at arm's length to the side. As soon as your dog looks away from the food and at you, he gets the cookie as a reward. **The look-at-me signal**: Say amiably, "Look" and immediately give your dog a treat, such as a Fresh. Soon your dog will look at you at you on this signal, awaiting the reward.

DOG'S DELI offers three recipes for training treats. Tuna Snaps and Fresh are also suitable for dogs who are allergic to wheat flour.

CHEESE STICKS

Ingredients	How to do it
2-1/2 cups (11 oz or 300 g) wheat flour 1/2 cup (2 oz or 50 g) oat bran 1/3 cup (2 oz or 50 g) semolina 3/4 cup (1/4 lb or 100 g) shredded Swiss cheese 1 egg 2 tablespoons (25 ml) sunflower oil About 1 cup (200 ml) water	1. Preheat oven to 300° F and line baking pan with baking paper. 2. Measure and mix wheat flour, oat bran and semolina. 3. Add the cheese, egg, sunflower oil and water. 4. Mix it all to a smooth dough with a hand or electric mixer. 5. Roll the dough about 1/4" thick on a floured surface. 6. Cut strips about 1/2" wide and 5" long with a large knife. 7. Twist the dough strips like corkscrews. 8. Put the cheese sticks on the baking pan and bake about 20 minutes at 300° F.
Utensils	
Rolling pin	

TIP Salt half the dough and use it to bake a tasty snack for yourself.

Variation
  You can also use other types of cheese, such as parmesan or Edam.

First baked on:

TUNA FISH SNAPS

Ingredients	How to do it
2-1/2 cups (9 oz or 250 g) rye flour 1/2 packet dry yeast (for 9 oz flour) 1 small can tuna fish (packed in water) 1 teaspoon dried rosemary 2 tablespoons (25 ml) olive oil About 3/4 cups (175 ml) warm water	1. Preheat oven to 320° F and line baking pan with baking paper. 2. Measure rye flour and mix with dry yeast. 3. Open tuna can and let the fish drip dry. 4. Add tuna, olive oil, rosemary and water to the flour. 5. Mix to a smooth dough with hand or electric mixer and knead by hand three more minutes. 6. Return dough to bowl with a bit more rye flour, cover with a dish towel, and let stand for 30 minutes. 7. Then knead the dough again and roll it about 1/4" (5 mm) thick on a floured surface. 8. Cut strips about 1/2" (1 cm) wide and 1 3/4" (4 cm) long with a large knife. 9. Place the strips on the baking pan and bake about 20 minutes at 320° F.

Utensils
Rolling pin, dish towel

TIP Rye flour is not very easy to work. The dough can stick quickly. If so, add a little more flour.

First baked on:

FRESH

Ingredients	How to do it
2-1/2 cups (14 oz or 400 g) rice flour 1 apple 1/2 cup (3.5 oz or 100 g) fat free yogurt 1 small bunch of fresh mint About 2/3 cups (150 ml) water	1. Preheat oven to 160 degrees C and line baking pan with baking paper. 2. Measure the rice flour and fat free yogurt. 3. Quarter the apple and puree it with the water. 4. Wash the mint and chop. 5. Mix it all to a smooth dough with a hand or electric mixer. 6. Make small nuggets with your fingers and put them on the baking pan. 7. Bake about 20 minutes at 320° F.
Utensils	
Hand mixer	

TIP: You can find rice flour in a well-stocked Asian food store.

DOG'S DELI uses a Thai product. Dogs who are allergic to grains can eat these cookies, since the flour consists 100% of rice. Fresh is also a very low-fat treat.

First baked on:

SHOPPING AT THE MARKET

Friday is Market Day, and Billy loves it very much.

Many market people from Duesseldorf know him already, ever since he was small. When he was just a pup, he could not yet stay home alone. In front of the supermarket he probably would have been stolen because he was so cute. So we went shopping at the market, and he was always allowed to come along.

Billy remembers his childhood happily; I have often gotten that impression. At the flower stand he gets rose heads to tear up, at the vegetable stand a carrot, at the Austrian butcher a slice of liver cheese. Even the baker gives him a dry roll. And recently he was allowed to try noodles with tuna, made fresh at an Iranian snack bar. An exception, since the noodles are spiced.

What fun, so many friends with whom he can flirt, and who spoil him.

BILLY'S FLIRTING TIP
Shake a paw
Have your dog sit down at the beginning of the training. Hold a cookie before his chest in your closed hand. First he will probably try to reach the treat with his snout. But keep the cookie hidden in your hand until he tries to reach it with his paw.
As soon as the dog touches your hand with his paw, give him the cookie as a reward.

For the Friday cookie recipes we buy fresh fruit, vegetables, and fish.

GUSTAV'S FAVORITE

Ingredients	How to do it
2-3/4 cups (3/4 lb or 325 g) whole-grain wheat flour 1-1/2 cups (4.4 oz or 125 g) fine oatmeal 1/3 cup (2 oz or 60 g) goose fat or 1/4 cup (60ml) olive oil 1 apple 1 teaspoon dried thyme About 1 cup (250 ml) warm water	1. Preheat oven to 320° F and line baking pan with baking paper. 2. Weigh and mix flour and oatmeal. 3. Quarter the apple and puree it with water. 4. Add the pureed apple, goose fat and thyme to the flour mix. 5. Mix to a smooth dough with hand or electric mixer. 6. Roll the dough about 1/4" thick on a floured surface, and cut out goose-shaped cookies with cutter. 7. Put the cookies on the baking pan and bake about 20 minutes at 320° F.
Utensils	
Rolling pin, mixer, goose cookie cutter	

TIP Unusual cookie cutters can be found in well-stocked household shops or on the internet.

Variations

Commercially available goose fat always contains some pork fat. Many dog owners, as a matter of principle, do not feed dogs any pork products. You can also replace the goose fat with sunflower oil.

First baked on:

RED CANTUCCINI

Ingredients	How to do it
1-1/2 cups (7 oz or 200 g) wheat flour 1/2 cup (3.5 oz or 100 g) semolina 2/3 cup (1.8 oz or 50 g) coarse oatmeal 1-1/3 cups (3.5 oz or 100 g) ground hazel nuts 1 level teaspoon baking powder 3/4 cups (3.5 oz or 100 g) fresh beets, cut up 1-2/3 tablespoons (25 ml) sunflower oil About 1 cup (225 ml) water	1. Preheat oven to 320° F and line baking pan with baking paper. 2. Peel beets, cut up, cook soft in water for about 40 minutes, and let cool. 3. Puree the beets in water. 4. Measure and mix flour, semolina and oatmeal with baking powder. 5. Add beets and sunflower oil. 6. Mix to a smooth dough with hand or electric mixer. 7. Roll dough about 1/2" thick on floured surface, cut strips 1/2" wide and make a roll of each one. 8. Cut pieces 1/4" thick and put them on the baking pan. 9. Bake about 20 minutes at 320° F.
Utensils	
Cooking pot, mixer, rolling pin	

TIP To save time, buy frozen pureed beets at the supermarket.

First baked on:

YOGURT WITH FRESH FRUITS

Ingredients	How to do it
3/4 cup (7 oz or 200 g) fat free yogurt 1/4 cup (50 ml) milk 3 tablespoons coarse oatmeal 3/4 cup (75 g) sliced fresh fruit (such as apple, pear or banana) Handful of hazel nuts or walnuts, sunflower seeds or shredded coconut 1 tablespoon honey or maple syrup	1. Stir yogurt smooth with milk. 2. Add oatmeal. 3. Wash, peel and cut up fruit small, stir it in. 4. Add chopped nuts, sunflower seeds and honey.

Billy loves milk products very much. Sometimes he is allowed to lick what remains out of the yogurt container. A wonderful job for him.

First baked on:

Lucy+Billy

ON THE GO WITH HIS BEST GIRL FRIEND

Three-year-old Billy is at the best age for a dog. People, especially children and ladies who have dogs, are his great love. And he likes best to greet each one with a present.

His Saturday walk with his girl friend Lucy, a yellow Labrador female, is a great pleasure. And they both like the same things: swimming, tussling and eating.

Only eating can be a problem. I always say that every pig's ear that Billy tears up shows up on the scales. And that's why there are just cottage cheese and apples for a meal now and then.

Swimming with Lucy takes a lot of energy and lets a lot of fat melt away. So they both are inspired to do a lot of retrieving with dummies and treats.

BILLY'S HUNTING TIP
On the Trail of the Cookies
Searching is the most pleasant activity for many dogs. For example, make a little trail of cookies for your dog. Flat surfaces are best for beginners. Advanced dogs can sniff out traces of cookies even in leaves or on gravel. Food or a dummy can be dragged over the ground. Then let your dog find the trail and, at the end, find a treasure of "Indians".

For Saturday we offer you three recipes for low-fat cookies.

DOGS LIGHT

Ingredients	How to do it
2-3/4 cups (3/4 lb or 350 g) wheat flour 2 cups (7 oz or 200 g) oat bran 1 cup (7 oz or 200 g) cottage cheese 1 fresh pear 1 teaspoon cinnamon About 1/2 cup (100 ml) water	1. Preheat oven to 320° F and line baking pan with baking paper. 2. Measure and mix wheat flour, oat bran, and cottage cheese. 3. Quarter pear and puree with water. 4. Add pureed pear with cinnamon to the flour mix. 5. Mix to a smooth dough with hand or electric mixer; you may add warm water. 6. Roll dough 1/4" thick on floured surface and cut out small dogs. 7. Put cookies on baking pan and bake about 20 minutes at 320° F.
Utensils	
Rolling pin, dog cookie cutter	

Variation
Instead of a pear, you can use a carrot.

Billy is not fond of cinnamon. In that, he differs from other dogs. As with us people, much is a matter of taste. Try the recipe with cinnamon or replace it with the marrow of half a vanilla bean.

First baked on:

INDIANS

Ingredients	How to do it
2-1/4 cup (7 oz or 200 g) chick-pea flour 1 level teaspoon baking powder 1/4 lb (100 g) fresh chicken breast 1 tablespoon fresh parsley About 1/3 cup (75 ml) water	1. Preheat oven to 320° F and line baking pan with baking paper. 2. Cook chicken breast in water about 15 minutes and let cool. 3. Puree chicken breast with water. 4. Wash and chop parsley. 5. Measure chick-pea flour and mix with baking powder. 6. Add all other ingredients and mix to a smooth dough with mixer. 7. Roll dough 1/2" thick on floured surface. Cut strips 1/2" wide and roll each into a roll. 8. Cut discs 1/4" thick with a knife and put on baking pan. 9. Bake about 20 minutes at 320° F.
Utensils	
Cooking pot, mixer, rolling pin	

TIP   We found chick-pea flour by chance in a Japanese market. It is made in England for Indian tastes. It is a good base for cookie recipes intended for dogs who are allergic to grains.

First baked on:

POTATO CHIPS WITH PARMESAN

Ingredients	How to do it
1 lb (500 g) fresh potatoes 1/2 cup (2 oz or 50 g) grated parmesan	1. Preheat oven to 140° F and line baking pan with paper. 2. Brush potatoes under water. 3. Cut potatoes into thin chips with slicer or knife. 4. Put potato chips on baking pan; be sure they don't overlap. 5. Dry chips about 90 minutes at 140° F. 6. Sprinkle parmesan on the potato chips. 7. Dry the chips for another ten minutes. 8. Take the pan out of the oven and let the chips dry overnight.
Utensils	
Vegetable slicer or sharp knife	

TIP Store the chips in a linen bag, so they can continue to dry.

Variation
> You can dry any kind of vegetable, such as carrots or zucchini, and fruits such as apples or bananas.

First baked on:

Ninja

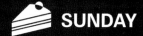

AFTERNOON GUESTS

Sometimes Sunday is a real holiday, when we await guests.

Billy sees Ninja again and we finally meet her owners. Ninja was already familiar with DOG'S DELI cookies before we opened. She was one of the testers in the first baking tests. And then she became famous for her portrait, which hangs behind the store counter.

Many customers say their dog looks just like Ninja. That would really be a very great coincidence. For Ninja's mother is a poodle-schnauzer mix. And her father? If only we knew!

Since a Labrador never welcomes a girl friend without a gift, we bake special treats, such as a Sunday cake with zucchini and Swiss cheese. To please the four-legged friends, this should be eaten up within the next four days, since its freshness is limited.

BILLY'S PLAY TIP

The Old Shell Game

Place three flowerpots on the floor upside down. In the absence of your dog, put an apple-cinnamon roll under one of them. Then let your dog try his luck!

If several dogs take part in the game, one can seek while the others practice **WAITING**.

For a visit, we offer the recipes for a Sunday cake, apple-cinnamon rolls and ruebli turnovers.

DINNER FOR TWO

SUNDAY CAKE

Ingredients	How to do it

4 cups (14 oz or 400 g) rye flour
2 level teaspoons baking
    powder
 	
1 medium zucchini
1-1/4 cup (4.4 oz or 125 g) Swiss
    cheese shredded
3 eggs
 	
2/3 cup (150 ml) milk
1/3 cup (75 ml) sunflower oil
	1. Preheat oven to 180 degrees C and grease bread pan with sunflower oil.
	
	2. Weigh rye flour and mix with baking powder.
	
	3. Wash zucchini and cut into small cubes.
	
	4. Weigh cheese and add eggs, milk, sunflower oil to other ingredients.
	
	5. Mix well and put dough in bread pan.
	
	6. Bake about 50 minutes at 180 degrees C. Stick a knife into the cake. If a little dough sticks to it, bake it a few more minutes.

Utensils	7. Let the cake cool ten minutes before you take it from the pan.
Small bread pan (about 30 x 11 x 7.5 cm)	

TIP   You can also make the Sunday cake as muffins. Then you have the right portions for dogs. Reduce the baking time to 25 minutes.

First baked on:

APPLE CINNAMON ROLLS

Ingredients	How to do it
4 cups (18 oz or 500 g) wheat flour 1 packet dry yeast (for 4 cups flour) 1/4 cup (50 ml) sunflower oil About 2/3 cup (150 ml) luke-warm water 1 small apple 1-1/3 cup (3.5 oz or 100 g) ground hazel nuts 1 pinch cinnamon About 1/2 cup (100 ml)water	1. Preheat oven to 340° F. 2. Measure wheat flour and mix with yeast. 3. Add sunflower oil and water to the flour. 4. Mix to a smooth dough with hand or electric mixer and knead dough another three minutes. 5. Put the dough back in the bowl with a little flour, cover with a dish towel, and let set 30 minutes. 6. Wash apple and puree along with hazel nuts, cinnamon, and water. 7. Then knead the dough again and roll about 1/4" thick on a floured surface. 8. Cut strips about 1/2" wide and 2" long and coat with apple-nut mixture. 9. Roll individual rolls and place them close together on the baking pan. 10. Bake the rolls about 20 minutes at 340° F.
Utensils	
Hand mixer, rolling pin	

TIP The apple-cinnamon rolls should not be kept longer than four days.

First baked on:

RUEBLI TURNOVERS

Ingredients	How to do it
2 cups (9 0z or 250 g) wheat flour 3/4 cup (3.5 oz or 100 g) sliced fresh carrots 1/8 cup (25 ml) sunflower oil About 1 cup (200 ml) water 1/2 cup (2 oz or 50 g) cubed ham 2 teaspoons chopped parsley	1. Preheat oven to 340° F. 2. Measure wheat flour. 3. Cut carrots into discs and puree in mixer with water and sunflower oil. 4. Combine all ingredients and mix to a smooth dough with hand mixer. 5. Roll dough about 1/2" thick on a floured surface. 6. Cut squares about 1/2" wide and fold into triangles. 7. Put turnovers on baking pan and bake about 20 minutes at 340° F.
Utensils	
Hand mixer, rolling pin	

Billy does not care much for fresh carrots. He likes practically anything in turnovers. One starts Labrador pups on ham. He likes it only in limited quantities, since the ham is salty.

First baked on:

RECIPE INDEX

Apple
Young dogs love apples, play with them first and then gnaw them up.

Banana
A banana is rich in starch and potassium, a great source of energy.

Carrots
Fresh carrots are healthy for pups to chew on.

Egg
Now and then Billy may eat a boiled egg and its shell. Great fun for him.

Fast Day
A fast day is not necessary for reasons of nourishment physiology.

Hunger
Billy is always hungry. Many other dogs resemble him in this way.

Joy
Our tail-wagging four-legged friends bring joy to us every day.

Juggling
At DOG'S DELI a dog can juggle a treat on his nose. Only at his master's command does he throw it in the air, catch and eat it. Very impressive.

Thirsty
Cookies make dogs thirsty, so always have enough water available.

Nosework
Nosework is a great pleasure for every dog. They have reasons for having a better sense of smell than people.

Oops
Oops! Another cookie fell off the counter. Billy is happy.

Oven
Every oven works differently. When you bake according to a recipe, check the cookies a few minutes before the end of the baking time cited in the recipe. They may be finished sooner.

Plum
Plums have a laxative effect. The pits may not be eaten.

Potato
Raw potatoes are unbearable. Cooked potatoes are a very digestible and albumin-rich food.

Yogurt
Yogurt and thick milk are preferable to other milk products because of their lower lactose content.

Rosemary
You can conserve dog cookies naturally with rosemary. But not every dog likes to eat it.

Storage
Store your fresh cookies best in a tin container or cloth bag. Thus they can continue to dry and last longer.

Street Dogs

They love our cookies particularly. They don't smell like dog food, but like human food, which street dogs must often survive on.

Sugar

As a matter of principle, sugar should not be fed to dogs. It is bad for their teeth and makes them too fat.

Teeth

Very hard baked treats help promote clean teeth.

Temperament

Temperamental dogs use up more energy than phlegmatic ones do. It is no wonder that we rarely see fat terriers at DOG'S DELI.

Vitamin C

Dogs can produce vitamin C in their own organs, so it does not need to be fed to them.

Whelp

We offer whelps only low-fat cookies in their first weeks of life.

Yorkshire

Yorkshire terriers love our cheese cookies and liverwurst croissants most. Big and hard cookies are not their first choice.

Billy

Thomas

Christiane

THANKS

The DOG'S DELI Team says "thank you" to all friends, partners and clients.

And above all, to the many dogs who cheer us every day and thus show us why we bake, decorate and develop new ideas from the heart every day.

Friederike

Simone

Jutta

Martina

Peter

Vera

NOTES

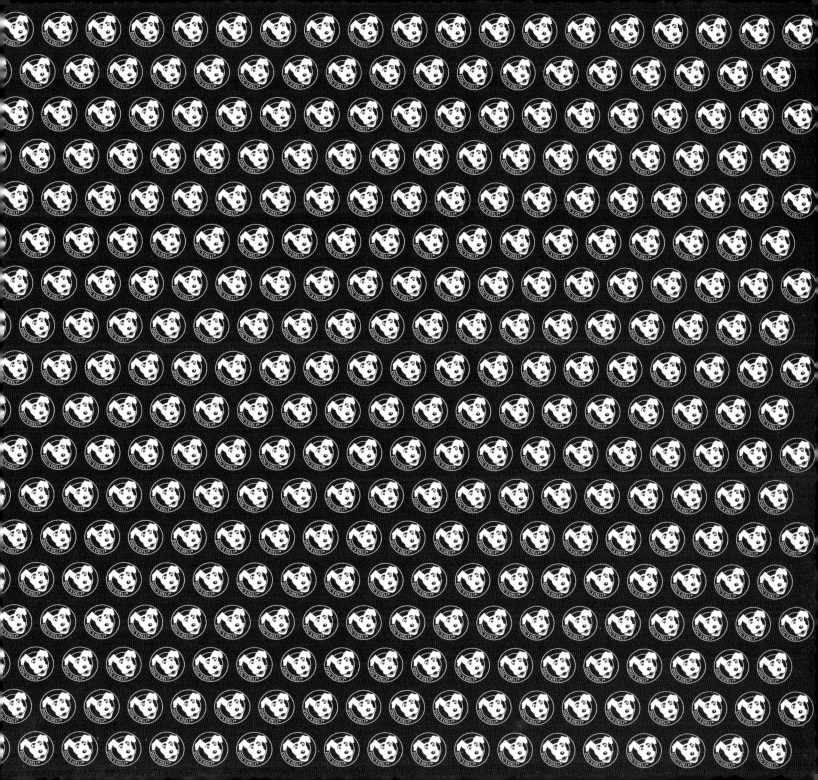